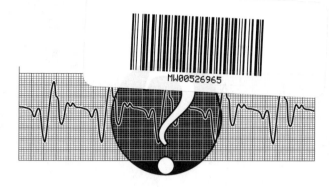

God's Life-changing Answers to

SIX VITAL
QUESTIONS
OF LIFE

PASTOR CHUCK SMITH

THE WORD
FOR TODAY

P.O. Box 8000, Costa Mesa, CA 92628
(800) 272-WORD (9673)
Web site: www.twft.com
E-mail: info@twft.com

Six Vital Questions of Life
by Chuck Smith
Copyright © 2004
Published by The Word For Today
P.O. Box 8000, Costa Mesa, CA 92628
1 (800) 272-WORD (9673)

Web site: www.twft.com
E-mail: info@twft.com

ISBN 1–932941–08–8

TABLE OF CONTENTS

INTRODUCTION 5

CHAPTER 1
What shall we say to these things?
Romans 8:31a 7

CHAPTER 2
For if God spared not his own Son...how much more
shall He not freely give us all things?
Romans 8:32 15

CHAPTER 3
Who shall lay any thing to the charge of God's elect?
Romans 8:33 23

CHAPTER 4
Who is he that condemneth?
Romans 8:34 29

CHAPTER 5
Who shall separate us from the love of Christ?
Romans 8:35 39

CHAPTER 6
Keep yourself in the love of God.
Jude 21 61

CHAPTER 7
What shall we say to these things?
Conclusion 71

INTRODUCTION

The Apostle Paul asks and gives the answers to six vital questions in Romans 8:31-39 that revolutionized my entire Christian life. Contemplating Paul's questions produced a 180-degree turnaround in my relationship with God and put me in the winner's circle. My conversion experience was great, but as I discovered the answers to these six questions, the change in my life was so profound, it was almost like a second conversion!

As you study these questions—vital questions—and ponder them in your heart,

and you consider the biblical rational, I'm
certain that they will have the same effect in
you, as they had in my life, and will transform
your relationship with God.

CHAPTER 1

What shall we say to these things?

Romans 8:31a

After the question "What shall we say to these things?" the Apostle Paul asks a series of vital questions. Perhaps "these things" refers to what Paul has just said; that God has given us His Spirit to help us in our weakness, and that all things are working together for good, for us who love God and are called according to His purpose. Paul then says that God foreknew us and predestined that we should be conformed to the image of His Son, and He also called us, then justified us, and glorified us. Thinking of all that God has done for me,

"What can I say to these things?" God's love
and grace toward me is far beyond anything
that I could ever deserve, or merit. When I
think of what God has done for me, I can only
stand and praise Him because words are
totally inadequate. The worship is almost in
silence. The vocabulary of man is insufficient
to express the wonder of the grace of God.

In 2 Corinthians, Paul talks about being
caught up into heaven and says what he heard
was so glorious that it would be unlawful to
attempt to describe the experience in human
language. The same is so when we come to
that consciousness and awareness of God's
goodness and God's grace upon us. We are so
overcome and awed that we have no language
to express how much we appreciate God's
work, how much we love Him, and how
grateful we are for what He has done for us.

In my own walk with the Lord, when I came
to this place in Romans 8, my eyes were
opened to the grace of God in a way I had
never experienced. This has transformed my

relationship with God radically. I no longer relate to him on the basis of my goodness, which at best is variable, but on the basis of His goodness which is a constant. These six questions asked by Paul have brought me into a new dimension of faith and trust in God. I am now in a place of experiencing the blessings of God upon my life like I never dreamed possible.

Paul asks this series of questions in the book of Romans that exposes the richness of God's love and grace available to us.

GOD IS FOR YOU

If God be for us, who can be against us? Romans 8:31b

For a long time in my Christian experience, I had the misconception that God, in a way, was against me.

I grew up with a philosophy called positive reinforcement. When a child does something good, you reward him. When he is bad, you withhold the reward. Having that as a

philosophical base for my training in childhood, I carried that idea over into spiritual
things. I thought God rewarded me when I
was good and especially faithful in my
devotional life, but that He would withhold
those rewards if I had erred somewhere along
the line. I was seeking the blessings of God
predicated upon my faithfulness and goodness. Yet, knowing that I often failed, I never
expected God to bless me. I felt that I didn't
deserve the blessings that I desired of the
Lord, and thus, I didn't have the faith to
believe that God would bless me. Deep down
inside I knew that there were flaws in my
Christian walk and in my relationship with
God, and so I did not expect God's blessing at
all—and worse, I thought that God was against
me!

I felt that God was waiting for me to make a
mistake, just so He could teach me a lesson by
bringing His judgment upon me. I believed
God was responsible for every bad thing that
had happened to me and He was punishing

me for some wrong I had done. After all, I knew I deserved it. I thought that I had to earn God's approval. Somehow I had to persuade God to love me, because the love of God was something that I had to earn. I thought God loved good boys and hated bad boys, like that song about Santa Claus "making a list and checking it twice, going to find out who's naughty and nice." I thought that He was keeping a list on me and checking it over, and my rewards and punishments would result from my actions. I did not comprehend the extent of God's love for me, that He could love me as much as He did, in spite of my faults. I had no understanding of grace and I felt that I had to earn blessings from God.

And then reading the first part of Paul's question, "If God is for us…" touched me. God is for me. God is not against me. In Romans 8:26, we see that God gives me His Holy Spirit to help me in my weaknesses. In verse 29, God has predestined that I should be conformed to the image of Jesus Christ, and has provided all that is necessary to accomplish that. God is for me! He wants me to live victoriously and has provided all that is necessary for a life of victory. God is not against me. What a revelation it is to know that God is for me!

SATAN IS AGAINST YOU

If God is for you, who can be against you? Satan is against you. He wants to rob you of the blessings that God desires to bestow upon you. He robbed me of those blessings for many years by pointing out my failures, my flaws, and by whispering, "How can you expect God to bless you when you're not really all that you should be as a child of God?" Satan wants to destroy you. He wants to lure you into self-destructive practices and habits. If you will look at your life and those things that have taken a grip upon your life—if you will be honest, you will recognize that these strongholds Satan has in your life are destroying you. Satan is after you and wants to destroy you. Who can be against us? Satan is against us. He will do everything within his power to keep you from following God completely, because Satan knows that God loves you and wants to bless you.

The blessings that we receive from God are predicated upon our faith to believe God to bless us. If I think that God won't bless me, then I don't have the faith to be blessed. However, if I understand that God wants to lavish His love upon me, then I learn to trust God to bless me, though I know that I'm not worthy or deserving of those blessings. That's what grace is all about, undeserved blessings.

Though Satan is against us, we must believe and trust in God's Word, "Greater is He that is in us than he that is in the world" (1 John 4:4). We should never think of Satan as an opposite of God. He is opposed to God, true, but the two are in totally different ballparks. Satan is a created being; God is the Creator. God is supreme. Satan's powers are limited; God's powers are unlimited. And thus, if God is for me, Satan, though he may be against me, is nothing against God. Consequently, I then

have the confidence to believe that greater is
He that is in me than he that is in the world.

CHAPTER 2

*For if God spared not His own Son. . .
how much more shall He not freely
give us all things?*

Romans 8:32

When Satan is hassling you concerning God's love, look at the cross where God displayed how much He loved you.

For if God spared not His own Son but delivered Him up for us all, how much more shall He not freely give us all things? Romans 8:32

Paul earlier said that God demonstrated His love for us in that while we were yet sinners, Christ died for the ungodly.

John wrote,

"In this was manifested the love of God toward us, because that God sent His only begotten Son into the world, that we might live through Him. Herein is love, not that we loved God, but that God loved us, and sent His Son to be the propitiation for our sins" (1 John 4:9-10).

Jesus tells us,

"For God so loved the world that He gave His only begotten Son, that whosoever would believe in Him would not perish, but have everlasting life" (John 3:16).

HOW MUCH MORE

If you are prone to question or doubt God's love for you, all you have to do is look at the cross, and there you see the demonstration— not only the fact that God loves you, but how much God loves you. "God so loved the world that He gave His only begotten Son."

Paul tells us here that God did not spare His own Son, but delivered Him up for us all. How much more then shall He freely give us all things? This argument goes from the greater to the lesser. God has already given to you the greatest gift He could possibly give— His only begotten Son. We can't really comprehend that.

Paul said,

"For a good person one might die. But God showed His love for us in that while we were yet sinners Christ died for the ungodly" (Romans 5:7-8).

The argument is: If God already has demonstrated His love by sending His Son to die for your sins, how much more then shall God freely give to you whatever your needs might be? All of our needs today are insignificant to the ratio of what God has already demonstrated in His willingness to give to you.

Sometimes we come hesitantly to God and say, "Well, Lord, I know it's an awful lot to ask, and I even hesitate asking, Lord, but would You possibly consider...." We think that we're asking some big thing, when in reality God has already said, "I love you so much that I'm willing to give My best for you." You don't have to beg God or try to persuade Him. How much more shall He then not freely give us all things?

Jesus said,

"If you being evil know how to give good gifts to your children, how much more shall your Father which is in heaven give good things to those that ask Him?" (Matthew 7:11).

Jesus turns it around. "You fathers (being the lesser) delight to give good things to your children, how much more will your Heavenly Father (being the greater) give good things unto His children who ask Him?"

Paul goes from the greater to the lesser—if God gave His Son (the greater), the rest is nothing compared to what God is willing to give (the lesser).

IN CHRIST JESUS
Think of what you need right now from

God. In your own life and situations, what is it that you desire from God? Remember this—God has demonstrated His willingness to give you whatever you need. Your need right now pales in comparison with what God has already given you, by giving His only begotten Son.

When Paul wrote to the church in Ephesus, he opened the letter with thanksgiving to God, for blessings that God had already given him.

> "Thanks be to God, the Father of our Lord Jesus Christ, who has blessed us with all spiritual blessings in Christ Jesus" (Ephesians 1:3).

The key words are "in Christ Jesus." All the blessings that God has for you, come to you through Jesus Christ—in Him, by Him—it's all in Christ. God provides all His gifts for you, in and through Jesus Christ.

In the first chapter of Ephesians, Paul began to list those spiritual blessings that God has bestowed upon us.

"According as He has chosen us in Him before
the foundation of the world, that we should be
holy and without blame before Him in love:
Having predestinated us unto the adoption of
children by Jesus Christ to Himself, according
to the good pleasure of His will, to the praise
of the glory of His grace, wherein He has made
us accepted in the Beloved. In whom we have
redemption through His blood, the forgiveness
of sins, according to the riches of His grace;
wherein He has abounded toward us in all
wisdom and prudence; having made known
unto us the mystery of His will, according to
His good pleasure which He has purposed in
Himself: That in the dispensation of the
fullness of times He might gather together in
one all things in Christ, both which are in
heaven, and which are on earth; [even] in Him:
In whom also we have obtained an inheritance"
(Ephesians 1:4-11a).

We are chosen in Him. God adopts us as His
children. We are accepted in the Beloved. We
have redemption through His blood, in Whom
we have obtained an inheritance. All of these

things—being chosen, adopted, accepted, redeemed, given an inheritance—are all in and by and through Jesus Christ.

Therefore, what we need is more of Jesus! We used to sing, "I want more of Jesus, more and more and more. I want more of Jesus than I ever had before." How true that is. If you have Jesus, you have it all. It's all wrapped up in Him, through Him, and by Him.

When I think of all the wonderful things that God has given to me, I realize that, first of all, God has given to me His only begotten Son, and then through Jesus, all of these other spiritual blessings have become available.

CHAPTER 3

Who shall lay any thing to the charge of God's elect?

Romans 8:33

Since I am in a place of public prominence, there are accusers who make charges against me. You expect that. When you are before the public, people will disagree with you and even hate you. I get my fan mail from them quite often, as they express their disagreements, including all kinds of lies about me. People who don't really know me propagate these lies, and then somehow use them against me.

Of course, the Apostle Paul said, "If I please all men then I'm not a servant of Jesus Christ"

(Galatians 1:10); so, it doesn't really bother me. This just proves that I'm on the right track in serving the Lord. I know that when I express an opinion, some will disagree with it. Even if I were perfect, which I'm not, there would still be those who would be making charges against me.

Jesus said, "A servant is not greater than his lord" (John 13:16). So I look at Jesus—as perfect as He was, in His day they slandered Him and even crucified Him. Today it continues. People still say horrible things against Jesus. I would not be surprised that if Jesus appeared on the scene today and began to come against the religious orders, as He did in His day, that they would crucify Him again. And here He is, perfect, yet they charged Him with all kinds of spurious things.

Though people might charge me with different things, I know there's One who is not laying any charge against me, and that's God. I take comfort in that. Who then is bringing charges against you?

In Revelation 12:10, John heard a loud voice from heaven saying,

> "Now is come salvation, and strength, and the kingdom of our God, and the power of His Messiah: for the accuser of the brethren is cast down, which accused them before our God day and night."

Who brings charges? Satan!

In the book of Job, we find Satan acting as the accuser of the brethren. In Job 1 beginning with verse 6 we read,

> "There was a day when the sons of God were coming to present themselves before the Lord, and Satan also came with them. And the Lord said to Satan, 'Where have you come from?' And Satan answered the Lord and said, 'From going to and fro throughout the earth, walking up and down in it.' And the Lord said to Satan, 'Have you considered My servant Job? There is none like him in the earth, a perfect man and upright, one who fears God and hates evil.'"

God gave Satan an evaluation of Job. God said, "He's a perfect man. He loves Me. He hates evil."

And Satan answered the Lord,

"Does Job fear You for nothing? Have You not put a hedge around him, and about his house, and about all that he has on every side? Aren't You watching over him and protecting him? You've made this hedge around him. You've blessed the work of his hands. He's a rich man. Put forth Your hand now, and touch all that he has, and he will curse You to Your face" (Job 1:9-11).

Satan accuses Job of really being a mercenary. "He doesn't really love You. He loves all the goodies that You give to him. Who wouldn't love You, if You blessed him as You've blessed Job?" And so Satan is accusing Job before God.

JUSTIFIED

It is God that justifies. Romans 8:33b

Justifying you is the exact opposite of

charging you. Justifying you dismisses the charges. God has declared that you are innocent. God has exonerated you from any charges that are made against you. It doesn't matter what anyone else thinks of you. He is the One that really counts. What does God think of you? That's what is important.

But how can God justify us? Jesus Christ took all of the charges that were once against us and paid the price, that we might be justified from those charges.

> God made Him to be sin for us, who knew no sin, that we might be made the righteousness of God through Him (2 Corinthians 5:21).

Many times our enemies lay charges against us—even our friends do. Certainly Satan likes to make charges, but it is wonderful to know that God is not laying any charges against us. It is God who has justified us.

The psalmist said, "Oh how blessed is the man to whom God does not impute iniquity" (Psalm 32:2). This means God does not have any list of charges against you. God does not put iniquity to the account of you, who are in Christ Jesus, walking after the Spirit. If you stumble and fall, God doesn't even keep a record of it. You are in Christ Jesus.

CHAPTER 4

Who is he that condemneth?

Romans 8:34

Satan constantly condemns me. Every time I fail to do something that I know I should have done, Satan comes in with heavy condemnation. Anytime I do something that I shouldn't have done, he condemns me again. I often condemn myself, as I realize I can't live up to the standards that God has set for me. I condemn myself for my shortcomings. But I'm thrilled for the fact that there is one who is not condemning me; that is Jesus.

JESUS MAKES INTERCESSION

It is Christ that died, yea rather, is risen again,

and is even at the right hand of the Father making intercession for us. Romans 8:34

Answering his own question, Paul said, "Jesus Christ isn't condemning you; He died for you. In fact, He's risen again from the dead and is at the right hand of the Father making intercession for you." Rather than condemning you, Jesus is interceding for you.

Far from condemning me, Jesus is doing the opposite. He is before God interceding on my behalf.

John wrote,

"My little children, these things I write unto you, that you sin not. If any man sin, we have an advocate with the Father, Jesus Christ, the righteous" (1 John 2:1).

I have an advocate representing me. My attorney speaks on my behalf before the Father. And Who is that? Jesus Christ. He is not condemning me, but He is an advocate on my behalf.

JESUS DOESN'T CONDEMN

When Jesus was talking with Nicodemus in John chapter 3, He said that God did not send Him into the world to condemn the world but that the world through Him might be saved. Jesus said, "He who believes in Me is not condemned" (John 3:18).

This reminds us of the first verse in Romans 8 which states,

"There is therefore now no condemnation to those that are in Christ Jesus, who walk not after the flesh, but after the Spirit" (Romans 8:1).

But Jesus went on to say,

"He that believes not in Me is condemned already, because he has not believed in the name of the only begotten Son of God. And this is the condemnation, that light has come into the world, but men love darkness rather than light, because their deeds are evil" (John 3:18-19).

When a man speaks against Jesus Christ, he is doing so because he is an evil man who loves darkness rather than light.

You remember the story of the woman that the Pharisees brought to Jesus. They declared that they had caught her in the act of adultery and condemned her by saying to Jesus, "Our law says we're to stone her. What do you say?"

Jesus replied, "I say unto you, whichever one of you is without sin, you throw the first stone." Then as He wrote on the ground, they each became convicted and began to walk away, until none was left. Jesus stood up, looked at the woman, and said, "What happened to your accusers?"

She said, "Well, sir, I guess I don't have any."

We remember those comforting words when Jesus said, "Neither do I condemn thee."

"You see," Jesus said, "I didn't come to condemn the world. I came to save the world." The world did not need condemnation; it was already condemned. He didn't come to condemn the world because it was already condemned. Jesus came to save the world. Because of the salvation He would provide, He could say those beautiful words to this woman taken in adultery, "Neither do I condemn thee. Go thy way and sin no more" (John 8:4-11).

SATAN CONDEMNS

Satan is always condemning us. Every time you stumble, he is there pointing an accusing finger at you and condemning you. He constantly seeks to get you to focus on your weakness and failure, rather than upon God's strength.

Satan attempts to persuade us that we have to earn God's favor, continually reminding us that we don't deserve to be blessed by God or even to be saved. The problem is that Satan can often build a strong case against us for condemnation. But Jesus died for our sins. He rose again and is at the right hand of the Father making intercession for us. "There is therefore now no condemnation to those that are in Christ Jesus, who walk not after the flesh, but after the Spirit" (Romans 8:1).

GENTLE CONVICTION

When we fall into sin, the Holy Spirit convicts us, gently saying, "Now, that wasn't right. You shouldn't have responded that way. You reacted in anger out of your own flesh." That isn't condemning; that's convicting.

When the Holy Spirit is working in our hearts, He is conforming us into the image of Christ by pointing out those places where we need improvement. The net effect of the Holy Spirit's conviction is that we can't wait to confess our sin to Jesus and to receive that cleansing.

John said,

"If we say we have no sin, we deceive ourselves and the truth is not in us. But if we confess our sins, He is faithful and just to forgive us our sins and to cleanse us from all unrighteousness" (1 John 1:8-9).

The Holy Spirit makes me aware of my failures, and I can't wait to say, "Oh Lord, I'm so sorry. Please, Lord. I receive Your forgiveness now. Thank You, Jesus, for Your love and for the cleansing of my sin, and for Your forgiveness." I race to the cross.

SATAN'S TRICKS

Satan often comes to me and says, "You are a mess—you have failed so many times. You know, God ought to give up on you. There's no hope for you. You knew better than doing that, and yet you did it anyway. How can you ever expect God to do anything for you?" Satan starts laying all these charges on me.

I used to listen to him. I'd think, "Yeah, he's right; I really shouldn't pray. I really shouldn't expect God to do anything for me." And Satan would drive me away through this condemnation. I wouldn't feel like fellowshiping. I wouldn't feel like reading the Bible, or praying, because I really didn't deserve forgiveness. The purpose of Satan's condemnation was to drive a wedge between God and me. I learned that Satan is sneaky and tricky. That is his purpose—to show me my failures, to drive me away from the place of help. Now when he does that, I just smile and I say, "You're right, Satan. I am a mess, but Jesus died for messes like me. You don't scare me away from the cross, Satan, you only drive me to the cross, for there is my only hope."

BROUGHT TO THE CROSS

When you turn it around and say, "Yeah, you're right, I need Jesus and I need His help right now," and you start running to the cross, Satan soon gives up. He finds out that his scheme has been reversed on him, and rather than driving you away from the cross, it drives you to the cross. We can experience real peace when we remember the Scriptures.

> Submit yourselves therefore to God. Resist the devil, and he will flee from you. Draw near to God, and he will draw near to you (James 4:7-8).

Now, of course, the purpose of the Holy Spirit is to bring us to the cross. As the Spirit convicts us, He draws us to that place of forgiveness, cleansing, strength, and power found only in Jesus Christ.

So reflecting back to the beginning of the eighth chapter of Romans where it says, "There is therefore now no condemnation to those that are in Christ Jesus," and examining the question, "Who is he that condemns?" we realize that it is not Jesus. He is at the right hand of God, making intercession for us!

CHAPTER 5

*Who shall separate us
from the love of Christ?*

Romans 8:35

The subject of Christ's love is so rich, so
deep, that it is beyond our capacity to grasp.

In fact, Paul prayed for those in the church
at Ephesus,

"That Christ might dwell in your hearts by
faith; and that you, being rooted and grounded
in love, may be able to comprehend with all
the saints what is the breadth, the length, the
depth, and the height; and to know the love of
Christ, which passes knowledge" (Ephesians
3:17-19).

Paul is praying that you can know something that is unknowable; that is, the fullness of the love of Christ which passes human knowledge.

> Now unto him who is able to do exceedingly abundantly above all that we ask or think, according to the power that works in us. (Ephesians 3:20).

Paul is asking God to do the impossible for you, giving you a little bit of an understanding on the fullness of Christ's love for you—the length, the breadth, the depth, the height; to know the love of Christ that passes human knowledge.

Jesus said, "As the Father has loved me, so have I loved you" (John 15:9), and "Greater love has no man than this, that a man lay down his life for his friends" (John 15:13).

NO SEPARATION

> Shall tribulation, or distress, or persecution, or famine, or nakedness, or peril, or sword? Romans 8:35

Satan likes to use various difficulties that I might face in life to make me feel that I am separated from the love of Christ. When I go through heavy trials, Satan likes to say, "Well, if God really loves you than why would God allow this to happen to you?" Satan uses tribulations, distresses, and persecutions to make me feel that somehow God doesn't love me. Satan rationalizes that a God of love would not allow me to experience such pain and mental anguish.

In Psalm 115, David asked, "Why should the heathen say, 'Where is now their God?'" (Psalm 115:2). Often people resent your commitment to Jesus Christ. When something goes awry in your life, they like to torment you by saying, "Well, where is your God now?" A lot of times we may be wondering that ourselves, "Where was God when this happened?" "Why didn't God stop that?" "Why did God allow that?" We may begin to question the love of Jesus Christ when we experience painful circumstances.

DRIVEN TO CHRIST'S LOVE

As it is written for Thy sake we are killed all the day long; we are accounted as sheep for the slaughter. Romans 8:36

In fact, at the time Paul is writing this, he had already gone through tribulation, distress, and persecution. He had experienced nakedness and peril and the sword. He gives us a long list in 2 Corinthians 12 of the things that he suffered, but this couldn't separate Paul from the love of Christ.

Now Paul quotes David from Psalm 44:22, "Yea, for Thy sake we are killed all the day long; we are counted as sheep for the slaughter."

David was complaining about the problems that he was facing. Beginning with verse 9, he wrote,

"But You have cast us off, You've put us to shame; You do not go out with our armies. [Lord, You deserted us.] You make us to turn back from the enemy: and they, which hate us,

take our spoil. You have given us like sheep
ready to be slaughtered; and have scattered us
among the heathen. You sell Your people for
nothing and you do not increase our wealth.
You have made us a reproach to our neighbors,
a scorn and a derision to them that are round
about us. You make us a byword among the
heathen, a shaking of the head among the
people. My confusion is continually before
me, and the shame of my face has covered me,
for the voice of him that reproaches and
blasphemes; by reason of the enemy and the
avenger. All of this has come upon us; and yet
we have not forgotten Thee, neither have we
dealt falsely in Your covenant. Our heart is not
turned back, and neither have our steps
declined from Your way, though You have
broken us in the place of dragons, and covered
us with the shadow of death. If we have
forgotten the name of our God, or stretched out
our hands to a strange god; shall not God
search this out? For He knows the secrets of
the heart. Yea, for Thy sake we are killed all
the day long; we are counted as sheep for the
slaughter" (Psalm 44:9-22).

So here Paul is talking about the same kind of distresses that David seemed to be going through; sufferings that often cause our minds to challenge the love of God for us. It had seemed that David and Paul were being prepared for the slaughter; that for God's sake they are killed all the day long, counted as sheep for the slaughter. But all of these circumstances drive us to the Lord, because only God is able to help and deliver us from these things.

MORE THAN CONQUERORS

In all these things we are more than conquerors through Him... Romans 8:37

We are more than conquerors in all trials and tribulations.

What is it to be "more than a conqueror?" To be a conqueror is to win the battle. You have defeated the enemy and you are rejoicing in the victory. Being more than a conqueror is to experience victory when the battle is still raging, and to be excited and rejoicing even in the midst of the attack. You can be more than a conqueror because you already have the victory through Jesus Christ, knowing that through Him, victory is assured. Being more than a conqueror is rejoicing in the midst of the conflict—that is true victory!

We must remember that Jesus fought the battle and defeated the enemy almost two thousand years ago. When He cried from the cross, "It is finished," this is a cry of victory. Satan's powers were broken. Jesus triumphed over the forces of darkness that are against us.

In Colossians, Paul speaks of that victory where the Lord defeated our enemy.

And you, being dead in your sins...He has made alive in Him, having forgiven all your trespasses; blotting out the handwriting of ordinances that was against you...and took it out of the way, nailing it to His cross; and having spoiled the principalities and powers [that were against you], He made a show of them openly, triumphing over them. (Colossians 2:13-15).

Jesus made an open display of victory over Satan's powers. You that are in Christ enter into His victory. Oh, we're still in a battle to be sure. There are still perils, distresses, tribulations, and persecutions, but in all of these things we are more than conquerors because Jesus defeated the enemy. The only hold that Satan can have on you is a lie, which you allow.

Sometimes a person will open the door and allow Satan to have a tight grip on their life. But thank God through Jesus Christ we can have—and do have complete victory over Satan. It is ours; all we have to do is claim it.

When Joshua was coming into the Promised Land, the Lord said, "Every place you put your foot I have given it to you." Not "I *will give* it to you." but "I *have given* it to you." You see the Lord has already given it to you; all you have to do is go in and lay claim to it. You step out in faith. "Yes, I claim this victory!" "Yes, this is mine!"

You can claim victory over temptations and the powers of darkness, because Jesus spoiled these, triumphing over sin at the cross, making an open display of His victory.

PERSUADED

I am persuaded... Romans 8:38

That word "persuaded" is a very strong word. It expresses unwavering certainty. There is no question on this; Paul is convinced.

In 2 Timothy 1:12, Paul wrote to Timothy, "I know in whom I have believed, and am persuaded."

That is the same word again; it speaks of absolute certainty.

Have you committed your life to the Lord? Then you can have absolute assurance that the Lord is going to keep you. Have you committed the future unto Him? If so, then you can have absolute certainty that the Lord is going to work out any problem that you might face in the future.

A PREORDAINED PLAN

... neither death... Romans 8:38

Paul continues his list of things that cannot separate me from the love of God that is mine in Christ Jesus. Far from separating me from the love of God, death actually brings me into His very presence.

To the Corinthians, Paul says,

"We wish rather to be absent from this body that we might be present with the Lord" (2 Corinthians 5:8).

To the Philippians he said, "I find myself with mixed emotions, I have a desire to depart, and to be with Christ." He is not saying, "I would desire to depart and be asleep," as though we sleep blissfully until that day we will see Christ. No, "I would desire to depart and to be with Christ," as he says, "which is far better. Yet, I know that you still need me" (Philippians 1:23-24).

Paul, most likely, thought, "The Lord is

probably going to allow me to stay around awhile because I have not yet finished or 'apprehended that for which I was apprehended by Christ Jesus.'" This is a great phrase and an interesting concept!

Paul realized that God had a plan designed for his own life as He does for each of us. Writing to the Ephesians Paul said,

"You are His workmanship; you have been created together in Christ Jesus for the good works, that God has before ordained that you should walk in them" (Ephesians 2:10).

Paul is saying that God has already planned out the things that He would have you to do for Him. In the meantime God is working in you right now, as He is preparing you for the good works, which He has before ordained that you should accomplish for Him.

Looking back on my life at this stage, I can see how the hand of God was working, as He was preparing me for the good work that He had before ordained that I should accomplish for His glory. This didn't happen overnight. This experience has taken a lifetime. Even before I was born, God was preparing me. All the way through my life, even from early childhood, God was preparing me for the good work that He had before ordained that I should accomplish for His glory and for the Kingdom.

There were many times when I questioned the call of God to the ministry. The life of a pastor did not have all the glory it has now. There were distresses and tribulations. My family and I faced problems in the early years of the ministry that caused me to question the calling of God that I felt upon my heart. But now looking back, I can see those difficult times were all part of God's preparation for the work that He had ordained that I should accomplish. Even so, God is working in you because you are His workmanship.

To the Philippians, Paul said,

"I have not yet apprehended that for which I was apprehended of Jesus Christ" (Philippians 3:12).

When the Lord stopped Paul on the Damascus Road, He had already mapped out Paul's future. At the same time, a man named Ananias was praying in Damascus. The Lord told Ananias to go to the street called Straight and inquire at the house of Judas for a man called Saul [Paul]. Ananias, in a way, backed away and said, "Wait a minute Lord, don't you know this Saul is out to destroy me? He has come to imprison and kill the Christians that call upon Your Name."

The Lord reassured Ananias, "Saul is a chosen vessel unto Me and I will show him the things that he must suffer for My sake."

When the Lord called Paul, He knew all the sufferings that Paul would have to go through—the slanderings, the imprisonments, and the near-death beatings. The Lord had designed Paul's ministry in advance, even when Paul [Saul] was persecuting the Christians. So too, the Lord has a plan and a purpose for each of our lives. That doesn't mean that we are going to automatically accomplish those purposes. When the distresses come, we can either be faithful like Paul or walk away, but our reluctance to continue walking by faith thwarts the purposes of God.

Death did not separate Paul from the love of God. Death does not separate us from the love of God, but ushers us into His presence. In the early church many times as a believer was being martyred, he would turn to the executioner and say to him, "You are only ushering me into the presence of my Lord." Basically, what is death going to do? It will bring me right before the throne of Jesus. So, can death separate me from the love of Jesus? No, of course not! It ushers me right into His very presence.

LIVE FOR CHRIST

...nor life... Romans 8:39

Many times it is harder to live for Christ than it is to die for Christ. Many people have a problem living for Jesus Christ. With the proper outlook, all of the trials and hardships that we go through in life are designed to bring us closer to Him, recognizing our reliance upon Jesus Christ. Life's difficulties and pressures bring us closer to God and help us to understand His loving purpose and plan for our lives.

L.E. Maxwell in his book titled, *Crowded to Christ* reminds us that God often puts us in a corner, closes every avenue of escape, except for Himself. The pressure is on so that we are crowded to Christ. In other words, when we're under pressure, we are pushed into Christ because we have no other place to go. Even though we come unwillingly, we still experience the help and victory of the Lord, and experience a greater awareness of His love.

SPIRITUAL WARFARE

...nor angels... Romans 8:38

Now Paul gets to the "who" in the question, "Who shall separate us?" No doubt this is a reference to the fallen angels.

Paul informs the Ephesians that we are in warfare, not wrestling against flesh and blood, but wrestling against principalities and powers—spirit forces that are in high places. Consequently, we need to have the whole armor of God that we might be able to stand against these forces, which are adverse to us.

We know that angels are divided into two categories. There are the angels that remained loyal to God and are called ministering angels, who are sent forth to minister to the heirs of salvation; on the other hand, there are evil angels that did not keep their first estate, and joined Satan and his rebellion.

The Bible says,

"For He shall give his angels charge over you, to keep you in all thy ways. They shall bear you up in their hands, lest you dash your foot against a stone" (Psalm 91:11-12).

There have been occasions when people have seen angels that appear as men, and some-times they appeared as angels. For example, when Peter was in prison, the angel of the Lord came and delivered him out of the prison. The angel woke him up and said, "Put on your sandals and follow me." The doors of the prison opened of their own accord, and the angel led Peter out of prison into the streets. Peter thought it was all a vision until it started to get a little chilly and then he realized that it wasn't a vision, but that he was really free!

I have never seen my angel, but I do believe that there is one, and I'm sure I've kept him busy.

At one time my brother, Paul, and I each had little '38 Fords. One rainy night we were going over to Hacienda Heights, on what was then only a two-lane road. You could say, we were racing each other as boys often do. As we began the race, Paul passed me and then quickly passed the car in front of me. I was trying to catch up and pulled out from behind this car to pass, when suddenly a car came from the other direction. I was going too fast to brake, but didn't want to rear-end the car in front of me. I pulled back in, but I was too close. I thought the mud on the side of the road would be softer than the metal on the car in front of me, so I chose to go to the side and take the consequences in the mud. As soon as I hit the mud, I began to slide out of control, and I slid right past the car in front of me—and right past my brother's car! He had slowed down, certain that I would be in a serious wreck. As I passed him, I eased back onto the road. I don't know how I ever managed that. In fact, I know I didn't. I know that there was an angel right there saying, "Fool, slow down and don't make me work so hard!"

I am also convinced that there are fallen angels opposed to us, and that we do face these angels in spiritual conflict. The question is: Can these fallen angels separate me from the love of God in Christ? The answer is no!

PRINCIPALITIES NOR POWERS

...nor principalities, nor powers... Romans 8:38

Principalities and powers seem to describe a ranking of angelic beings; you might say they are like lieutenants and captains. They are, more or less, a ranking of angelic beings, according to authority, who are good and bad. Paul wrote to the Ephesians, "We do not wrestle against flesh and blood, but against principalities and powers." And we have already referenced Colossians 2 where Christ, on the cross, destroyed the principalities and powers that were against us, triumphing over them through His death on the cross.

PRESENT AND FUTURE

...nor things present... Romans 8:38

As I look around my life today, I can't see anything presently that can separate me from God's love.

...nor things to come... Romans 8:38

Trying to think of what might happen in the future—what sorrows, what difficulties, what problems I might face—I'm certain that there is nothing that the future holds for me that can separate me from the love of God that is in Christ Jesus.

HEIGHT NOR DEPTH

Nor height, nor depth... Romans 8:39

These could be considered as astrological terms. Astrology goes way back to Babylon, and later became very popular during the time of Rome. Even today in this enlightened age, people still believe that the stars have some kind of mystical power, so that the date of your birth determines which of the stars are having an influence upon you. Some people believe during the time of your rising star that you must take action. Then as the year goes by and your star begins to set, they believe you should close your doors and stay inside. The idea that the stars exert some kind of mystical force is a bunch of foolishness.

Apparently, Paul is referring to the notion that some believed in the effect of stars rising and falling, when he says, "nor height, nor depth"—these things cannot affect God's love for you.

CREATED THINGS

...nor does any other created thing...
Romans 8:39

We have been talking about spirits, which are a realm of beings created by God. They can't separate me from the love of God in Christ, nor any other created thing. There may be other created things, that we don't know anything about, that God has not mentioned in the Bible. There could be, but we don't know. Unless the Bible told us about angels, we really wouldn't know much about them.

So, if there be any other created thing, whatever it is, it can't separate me from the love of God which is in Christ Jesus.

...shall be able to separate us from the love of God, which is in Christ Jesus our Lord...
Romans 8:39

You can be reassured and secure in Jesus Christ, knowing that nothing can separate you from His love.

CHAPTER 6

Keep yourself in the love of God

Jude 21

As we look at the list that the Apostle Paul has given in Romans 8:31-39, he omits one thing. Paul leaves off of this list the only thing that *can* separate you from the love of God in Christ Jesus. That is you yourself. God has created us with volition, a will, and has allowed us self-determination.

It is interesting that Jude, in that little letter of his, exhorts us, "Keep yourself in the love of God" (Jude 21).

This exhortation would be totally meaning-less if I did not have the power to remove myself from the love of God. No outside force or experience can separate me from the love of God. However, I myself am the only one who can cause estrangement by choosing to turn my back upon God's love

Jude reminds us of those groups that failed to keep themselves in the love of God.

FEAR AND UNBELIEF

Jude first discusses the children of Israel, who, though God delivered them out of the bondage of Egypt, perished in the wilderness. Their hindrance was unbelief. God brought them to the borders of the Promised Land, but they refused to enter in because of fear and unbelief. Their lack of faith caused them to wander in the wilderness until that entire generation had died. They failed to keep themselves in the place where God, in His love, could do for them what He wanted to do.

Many people have been delivered out of Egypt, but unfortunately they have failed to press on into the Promised Land because of unbelief. And thus, they never experience the full blessing that God desires to bestow upon them because of His love for them.

REBELLION

The second group consists of the angels, who kept not their first estate and now are being reserved in the chains of darkness awaiting the Day of Judgment. These created beings of God actually were in the very presence of God, singing and worshiping together when God had laid the foundations of the world, yet, they failed to keep themselves in the love of God. When Satan, one of the chief angels, rebelled these angels chose to go with Satan's rebellion against God. They kept not their first estate.

Isaiah 14:13 tells us that Satan had said, "I will exalt my throne above the stars of God. I will sit in the congregation in the sides of the north," manifesting his prideful lust to be like the Most High God.

LUST

With Sodom and Gomorrah, it was their unbridled, ungoverned lust that kept them from the love of God and ignited the wrath of God, and it rained fiery brimstone from heaven destroying them all.

HATRED

One individual who failed to keep himself in the love of God was Cain. According to Jude, he allowed hatred to fill his heart and this hatred removed him from the place of receiving God's love. What was Cain's predicament? Basically, it was a hatred he had developed for his brother, Abel. Any time you allow hatred to master your life, you are removing yourself from the love of God. God can't bless you. God can't do the things that He wants to do for you when you are mastered by hatred.

GREED

Another who did not keep himself in the love of God was Balaam, that mysterious prophet. His downfall was greed. Ultimately, Balaam was destroyed, along with King Balak, because of the wicked advice he gave to the king, causing a stumbling block for God's people.

JEALOUSY

Then, of course, there was that fellow Korah, the Levite, who rebelled against Moses' authority. He was jealous over the position that God had given to Moses. Anytime you allow greed or jealousy to master your life, God cannot bless you. You have removed yourself from the love of God, the place of God's blessings upon you.

SPIRITUAL DEVELOPMENT

And beside this, giving all diligence, add to your faith virtue (2 Peter 1:5).

Notice Peter uses the word "add" which means to go forward. I fear many people are in a state of arrested spiritual development. They are in the same spiritual condition today as they were twenty-five years ago. There hasn't been any real spiritual development in their lives. As Paul said to the Corinthians, "You are still babes. At the time when you should be able to take some meat, you still need milk because you are a babe in Christ."

There is a time when being a baby is natural. It is exciting to hear your child say, "da-da" for the first time. I can remember when my daughter first said "da-da." Wow! It was glorious! But now if I were to walk into my adult daughter's room and all she said was "da-da," it would be painful. If she had not developed and was still only a baby in thought and actions, it would be heart-breaking.

I wonder if God experiences heartache when we don't develop. God must be grieved when we don't add to our virtue, knowledge; and add to our knowledge, temperance; and add to our temperance, patience; and to our patience, godliness; and to godliness, brotherly kindness; and to brotherly kindness—love.

For Peter continues to say,

"If these things be in you, and abound, they
will make you neither barren nor unfruitful in
the knowledge of our Lord Jesus Christ. But he
that lacks these things is blind, and cannot see
afar off [he is near-sighted], he has forgotten
that he was purged from his old sins.
Wherefore the rather, brethren, give diligence
to make your calling and election sure: for if
you do these things you shall never fall" (2 Peter
1:8-10).

If you are growing, if you are adding, if you
are developing, you are on the right track. You
will never fall as long as you are going forward.
It is only when you are standing still that you
are in danger of slipping backwards. I don't
think there is any real place for static
Christianity, a place where you are not going
forward in your Christian walk. So, it is
important for each of us to look at our lives
and ask the question, "Am I going forward in
my relationship with the Lord, or am I just
trying to maintain a status quo?" We each need
to consider this question seriously.

BUILDING UP YOUR FAITH

How do you keep yourself in the love of God? Jude gives the answer in verse 20,

"Build yourself up in the most holy faith."

There are many exercises for your faith. First, you can build up your faith by reading the Word. Faith comes by hearing and hearing by the Word of God. Listening to what God says in the Scriptures builds you up in the faith and keeps you in the love of God.

Secondly, Peter speaks of "Praying in the Holy Spirit" (Jude 20). This is done in three different ways that I know, perhaps there are more. One; you ask the Holy Spirit to guide your prayers. Two; through groanings which cannot be uttered.

Paul wrote in Romans 8:26,

"The Spirit helps our infirmity of not knowing how to pray as we ought: but the Spirit Himself makes intercession for us with groanings which cannot be uttered."

Three; by praying using the gift of speaking in an unknown tongue.

Again, Paul says in 1 Corinthians 14:14-15,

"If I pray in an [unknown] tongue, my spirit prays, but my understanding is unfruitful. What is it then? I will pray with the Spirit, and I will pray with the understanding also...."

Finally, we keep ourselves in the love of God by looking for that glorious day of the Lord when He will appear. Realizing that Jesus is coming soon helps to keep a proper perspective on worldly and material things. Paul said, "May your every contact with the world be as light as possible." Hang loose. Don't get anchored into the material things that are going to inhibit your growth in the things of the Spirit.

So, if you are maintaining a healthy spiritual walk with God, you will never be barren nor unfruitful, and if you will remain in Christ, you will never fall.

CHAPTER 7

What shall we say to these things?

Conclusion

It all leads back to the very first question—the one that introduces the six questions: "What shall we say to these things?" What can you say? God is for me. Jesus isn't condemning me. He loves me and He's interceding for me. Nothing can separate me from His love.

What shall we say to these things? I find that I'm quite speechless. What shall we say? Well, I often say, "Oh thank You, Jesus." I exclaim, "Glory!" I shout, "Praise the Lord." What can you say to these things? We have this wonderful, wonderful position of security and strength in Christ. What can you say? "Thank You, Jesus."

"There is therefore now no condemnation to those that are in Christ Jesus, who walk not after the flesh, but after the Spirit." This tells me that the only place I want to be is in Christ Jesus.

Paul said, "who walk not after the flesh, but after the Spirit." That is what I want!

Jesus spoke of abiding in Him, and His abiding in us (John 15:7). He then exhorted, "Abide in Me." That's my desire—to abide in Him, both now and forever. Abiding in Christ, this is the place of security and blessing.

If you are not in Christ Jesus, then you are already condemned. The death sentence has already been issued. The Bible said, "All of us have sinned and come short of the glory of God" (Romans 3:23). And it is declared that, "The wages of sin is death" (Romans 6:23). So, you're already condemned to death because of your sin, if you're not in Christ Jesus. This message of "no condemnation" does not apply to you; it is only applicable to those that are in Christ Jesus.

The question is: Are you abiding in Him? Does He abide in you? Are you in Christ Jesus today?

John said,

"If we confess our sins, He is faithful and just to forgive us, to cleanse us from all un-righteousness" (1 John 1:9).

Today you can be cleansed from all of the sin that has damaged and marred your life. Today you can begin a new life in Christ.

"For if any man is in Christ Jesus, he is a new creature. The old things have passed away, and everything is become new" (2 Corinthians 5:17).

Maybe Satan has been working overtime, sort of challenging you because of a difficult situation you might have right now. It's time for you to renew your faith in His promises.

Maybe you're not progressing and feel you are in a state of arrested spiritual development. You're not going forward and you realize that you're about in the same place that you were at this time last year—and come to think of it, probably at the same place you were five years ago. It may even be that ten years ago, you were closer to Jesus than you are today. You are in a dangerous place. You're going the wrong direction. Time to turn around and make your calling and election sure, as Peter said, and time to really get serious in the things of the Lord.

Father, we thank You that You have justified us. We thank You that Jesus Christ is there interceding for us. We thank You, Father, that You spared not Your own Son, but delivered Him up for us all, that You might demonstrate to us how fully You are willing to show us Your love and Your goodness and Your grace.

Father, for those that have been under condemnation by Satan's accusations, help them, Lord, to see the light. May they see that

You're not the one condemning them. You're not the one laying charges against them. And Lord, as we seek to follow You and to serve You, there's really no condemnation to those that are in Christ Jesus.

Lord, may we abide in Christ Jesus, realizing that He is the place of security, the place of blessing, the place of being justified. It is all in and through and by Christ Jesus our Lord. Thus, may we abide in Him. And Lord, we invite You to abide in us.

In Jesus' name. Amen.

OTHER TITLES BY CHUCK SMITH

THE MAN GOD USES
Item #: BKTMG01PB

Do you want to be used by God? In his warm personal style, Chuck Smith examines the personal characteristics of the people God used throughout the Scriptures. 144 pages.

MY STRONG TOWER
Item #: PAMST01

What is the name of God? Starting with Proverbs 18:10, Chuck Smith takes a close look at the names of God mentioned in the Old & New Testaments. 24 pages.

LIVING WATER
Item #: BKLWA01PB

This book captures the message of God's ability to change lives through His Holy Spirit. The reader will grow deeply in his knowledge and understanding of the Holy Spirit; His grace, His love, His power, and His gifts. 297 pages. Study guide available.

WHY GRACE CHANGES EVERYTHING
Item #: BKWGC01PB

Through remarkable insight gleaned from his own life, Pastor Chuck unfolds the mystery of grace and reveals many surprising truths. The reader will be refreshed and encouraged by the depth of God's grace toward us. 218 pages. Study guide available.

CALVARY CHAPEL DISTINCTIVES
Item #: BKCCD01

In Calvary Chapel we value both the teaching of God's Word, as well as the work of the Holy Spirit. This book explains the balance that makes Calvary Chapel a distinct and uniquely blessed movement of God. 250 pages. Study guide available.

HARVEST
Item #: BKHAR01PB

Recounting the growth of Calvary Chapel, this book features the life and testimonies of Chuck Smith and nine other Calvary Chapel pastors. God called these leaders, just as He has called you. Read this inspiring story of evangelism, discipleship and faith. 154 pages.

CHARISMA VS. CHARISMANIA
Item #: BKCVC01

Chuck Smith gives a scripturally balanced look at the person and work of the Holy Spirit. He carefully points out the difference between true charisma and the "charismatic experience." 142 pages.

EFFECTIVE PRAYER LIFE
Item #: BKCBA10

Practical studies in prayer that equip and help you to have a more effective and dynamic prayer life. An excellent resource for personal growth and group discipleship. 102 pages.

THE GOSPEL ACCORDING TO GRACE
Item #: BKTGA01

A clear and enlightening commentary on the Book of Romans. Chuck Smith reviews Paul's Epistle—one of the most important books in the Bible, on a verse-by-verse basis. 231 pages. Study guide included.

ANSWERS FOR TODAY
Item #: BKAFT01

This is a compilation of the popular Answer Pamphlet series in paperback form. It includes "The Rapture" "Be An Example," "God's Plan For The Ages," "A More Sure Word," and more. 247 pages.

THE FINAL CURTAIN
Item #: BKCBA12

This recently updated book deals with such subjects as Bible prophecy, the Middle East, and the role of the Antichrist. Also included is a helpful glossary with terms relating to the Bible and prophecy. 132 pages.

THE CLAIMS OF CHRIST
Item #: PATCO01

Chuck Smith gives a straightforward presentation of the claims of Jesus Christ, along with proof of their validity. Readers are challenged to accept or reject the Claims of Christ. 24 pages.

THE TRIBULATION AND THE CHURCH
Item #: BKTTA01

Will the church of Christ experience the Tribulation? This book expounds upon biblical prophecy and future events while looking at the church. 72 pages.

WHAT THE WORLD IS COMING TO
Item #: BKWTW01

What is the world coming to? The answer is documented in the Book of Revelation: a prophetic and unerring account of man's final days on earth. This book is a complete commentary on the book of Revelation and the scenario for the last days. 215 pages.

COMFORT, FOR THOSE WHO MOURN
Item #: PACFT01

In this pamphlet, Pastor Chuck shares the glorious hope we have in the resurrection of Jesus Christ and how we can find comfort through Him during a time of loss. 28 pages.

CALVINISM, ARMINIANISM & THE WORD OF GOD
Item #: PACAA01

This pamphlet discusses the facts upon which these two doctrinal stands are based, and compares them to the Word of God. 20 pages.

REDEMPTION
Item #: PARED01

In this clear and easy-to-read commentary, Pastor Chuck explores and explains the concept of our redemption in Christ using the story of Ruth and her "Goel,"or savior, Boaz. 24 pages.

For information about additional products, receiving a free product catalog, or to be added to our e-mail list for product updates, please contact:

THE WORD
FOR TODAY

P.O. Box 8000, Costa Mesa, CA 92628
(800) 272-WORD (9673)

Also, visit us at: www.twft.com
e-mail: info@twft.com